Scary Creatures
OCTOPUSES and SQUID

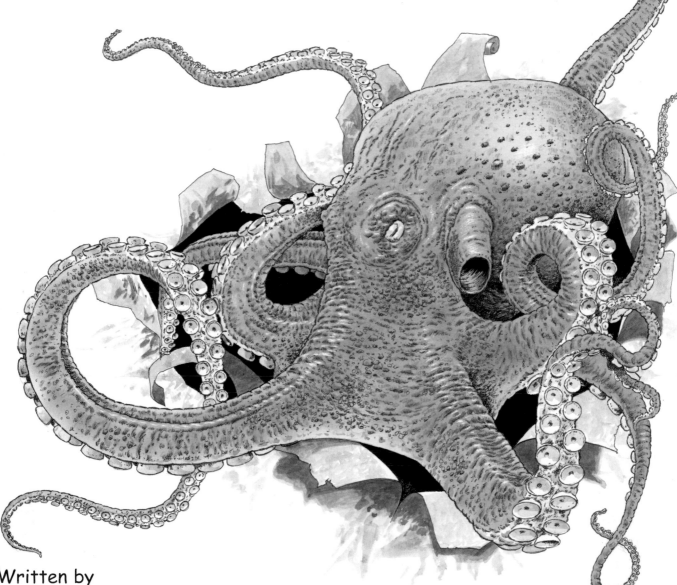

Written by
Gerald Legg

Illustrated by
Carolyn Scrace
John Francis

BOOK HOUSE

Created and designed by
David Salariya

Author:

Dr Gerald Legg holds a doctorate in zoology from Manchester University. He worked in West Africa for several years as a lecturer and rainforest researcher. His current position is biologist at the Booth Museum of Natural History in Brighton.

Artists:

Carolyn Scrace is a graduate of Brighton College of Art, specialising in design and illustration. She has worked in animation, advertising and children's fiction and non-ficton, particularly natural history.

John Francis is a leading natural history artist whose work can be found in many books, on greetings cards, prints, porcelain and calendars, as well as being featured in museums and zoos around the world.

Additional artists:

David Antram, Nick Hewetson, Mark Bergin

Series creator:

David Salariya was born in Dundee, Scotland. In 1989 he established The Salariya Book Company. He has illustrated a wide range of books and has created many new series for publishers in the UK and overseas. He lives in Brighton with his wife, illustrator Shirley Willis, and their son.

Editor: Michael Ford
Picture research: Matt Packer

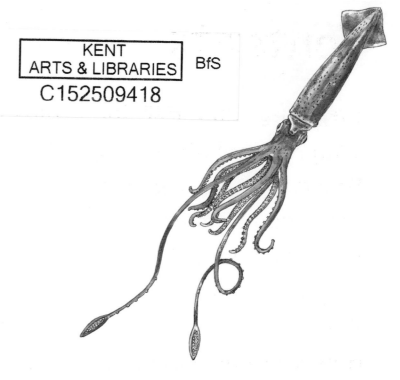

Photographic credits:

Agence Nature/NHPA: 6
Alex Kirstitch/Visuals Unlimited: 20
ANT photo library/NHPA: 14
Bill Wood/NHPA: 12
Corbis: 11, 17, 27
Daniel Heuclin/NHPA: 7, 13b
Linda Pitkin/NHPA: 18, 25
Mountain High Maps/©1993 Digital
 Wisdom Inc: 28-29
Norbert Wu/NHPA: 5
Peter Scoones/Nature Picture Library: 17
Richard Herrmann/Visuals Unlimited: 21
Trevor Mcdonald/NHPA: 13t

Published in Great Britain in 2004 by Book House, an imprint of
The Salariya Book Company Ltd
25 Marlborough Place, Brighton BN1 1UB

Visit the Salariya Book Company at
www.salariya.com
www.book-house.co.uk

A catalogue record for this book is available from the British Library.

ISBN 1 904642 22 5

Printed in China.

Printed on paper from sustainable forests.

Contents

What are octopuses and squid?

Octopuses and squid and their relatives, cuttlefish and the nautilus, are molluscs called cephalopods. This word means 'head-foot'. They have this name because their feet, or arms, are joined to their head. Around the mouth is a ring of tentacles armed with suckers. The foot also forms a special funnel, the siphon. This can be used to squirt water for jet propulsion.

Many cephalopods have large eyes and excellent vision. Like a chameleon they can also change colour to hide or to show how they feel.

Are jellyfish cephalopods?

A jellyfish does have a soft body like a cephalopod, but its tentacles are armed with stinging cells, while the arms of a cephalopod have suction discs.

No, a jellyfish is not a cephalopod.

Did you know?

Many kinds of octopus and squid live deep down in the oceans where it is icy cold and dark.

A deep-sea octopus

Why are cephalopods scary?

Their large eyes and long suckered arms make octopuses and squid appear strange and scary. There are many legends about these intelligent animals. Some octopuses and squid grow to a huge size and have been thought to sink ships and eat people.

Did you know?

The largest cephalopod is the giant squid. It is also called the colossal squid. It is a real sea monster and can grow to a total length of 12 m.

A deep-sea squid in the depths of the ocean

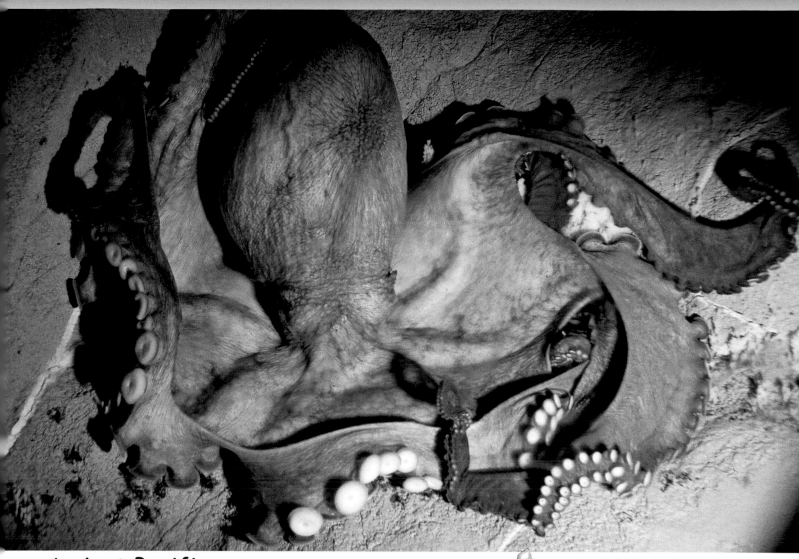

A giant Pacific octopus

The giant Pacific octopus (above) could have given Jules Verne his idea for the monstrous creature in his book, *20,000 Leagues Under the Sea.*

The Kraken

For thousands of years seafarers have told stories of monstrous many-armed sea creatures. The Kraken (right), a giant squid from a Norwegian legend, could sink large ships and drown sailors.

What's inside a cephalopod?

The body of a cephalopod is like a bag. Skin and muscle surround the internal organs, or 'visceral mass'. Apart from the nautilus, the visceral mass consists of two gills, two kidneys, a large liver, gonads, gut and three hearts. Its brain is protected inside a tough skull. An octopus's blood is blue because it contains copper.

Small is deadly. The blue-ringed octopus (below) is one of the most poisonous sea creatures. The smallest species weighs only 28 g and can even bite through a diver's wet-suit.

X-Ray Vision

Hold the page opposite up to the light and see what's inside an octopus.

See what's inside

poison glands

ink sac

brain

arm

beak

A blue-ringed octopus

siphon

sucker

arm

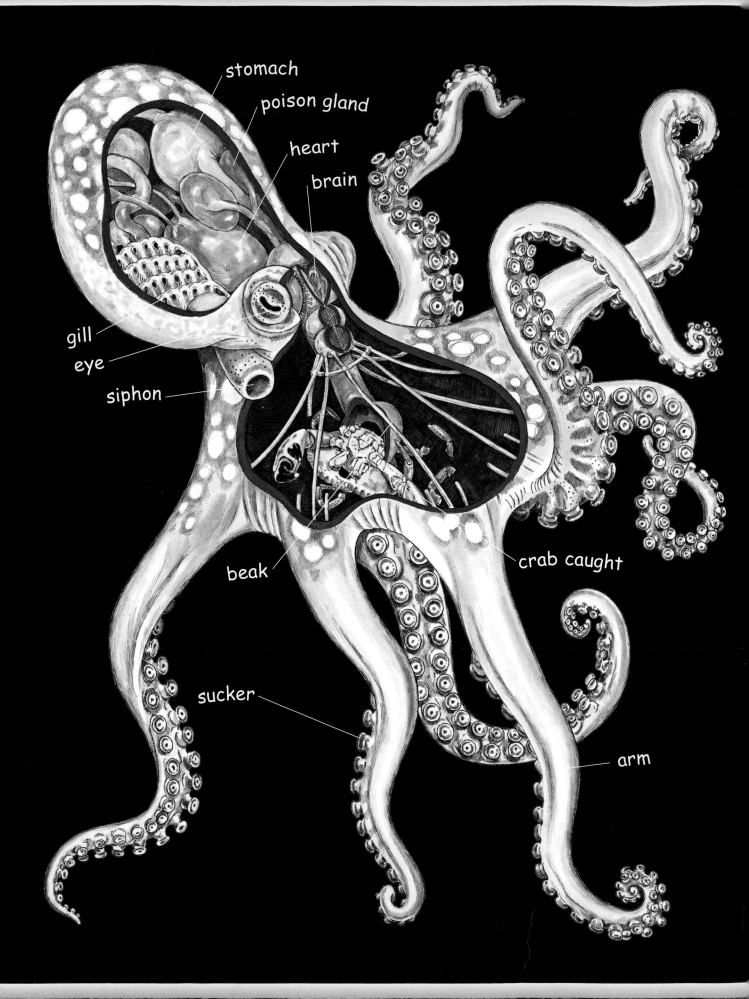

What do cephalopods eat?

Octopuses and squid eat all kinds of sea creatures, from tiny shrimps to 20-kg fish. The tips of the arms can reach into gaps in rocks in search of food. They grip their prey with their strong arms and disc-like suckers. Once caught, the prey is crushed by the beak. A 'tongue', the radula, scrapes the food and pushes the pulp into the mouth.

Did you know?

Common octopuses love to eat crabs. They float down onto them with outstretched arms. One octopus was seen eating 17 crabs in a single session.

An octopus eating a scallop

The beak is hard and sharp, made of the same material as a fingernail. It soon cracks open a scallop (above), exposing the soft meat inside.

Fish, crabs, prawns, lobsters, clams, mussels, limpets, worms, seaweed and even other squid and octopuses are all on the menu.

Are cephalopods good hunters?

Cephalopods use venom to immobilise their prey. Squid are fast-moving hunters, often working in shoals. Octopuses are more solitary. They are stealthy nocturnal hunters, exploring rocks in search of prey. They sometimes hide and wait for a victim to pass their lair.

When attacking its prey, a squid shoots out two special arms called tentacles. These grab the prey (below) and pull it backwards to be crushed by the beak.

Did you know?

Some deep-sea squid produce light on their tentacles to attract their prey.

A squid attacking its prey

An octopus parachuting onto its prey

With arms rolled back, an octopus descends onto its prey (above). It uses the web of skin between the base of each arm as a parachute.

Excellent vision helps make octopuses and squid good hunters. The powerful suckers (right) grip their victim. Cephalopods that feed mainly on fish have suckers armed with hooks to grip their slippery prey.

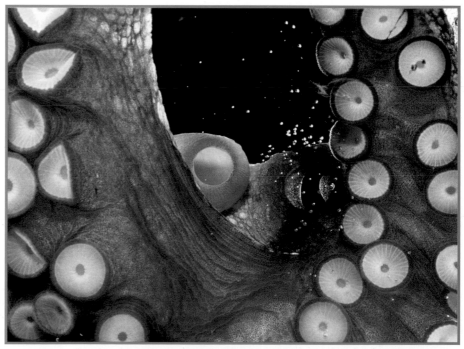

A close-up view of an octopus's eye, siphon and suckers

How do cephalopods swim?

Cephalopods move in water by jet propulsion. Water enters and expands the mantle cavity. The edges are sealed and the muscles of the mantle rapidly squeeze to force water out through the siphon. The pressure of the water as it is forced out pushes the animal forwards. By pointing the siphon, the animal can move in different directions.

Arms trail behind as a blue-ringed octopus jets away from danger (below). Octopuses have no internal skeleton to support their bodies.

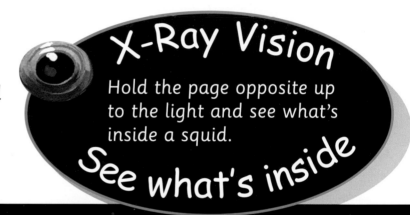

X-Ray Vision

Hold the page opposite up to the light and see what's inside a squid.

See what's inside

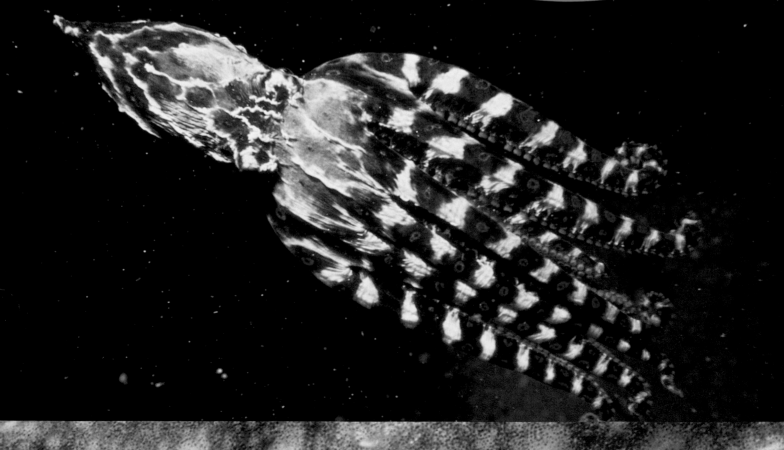

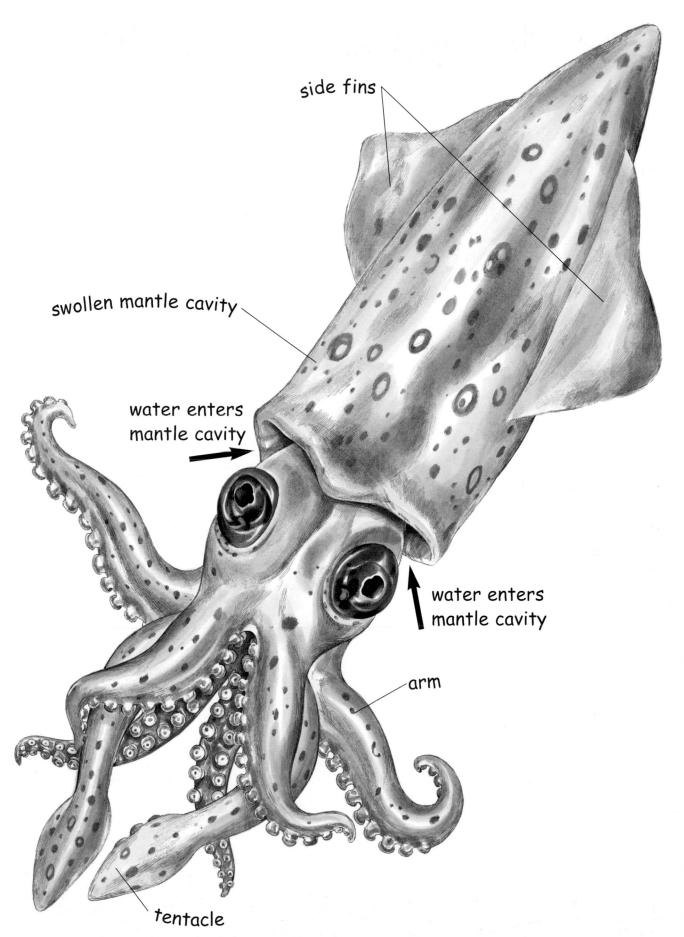

side fins

swollen mantle cavity

water enters
mantle cavity

water enters
mantle cavity

arm

tentacle

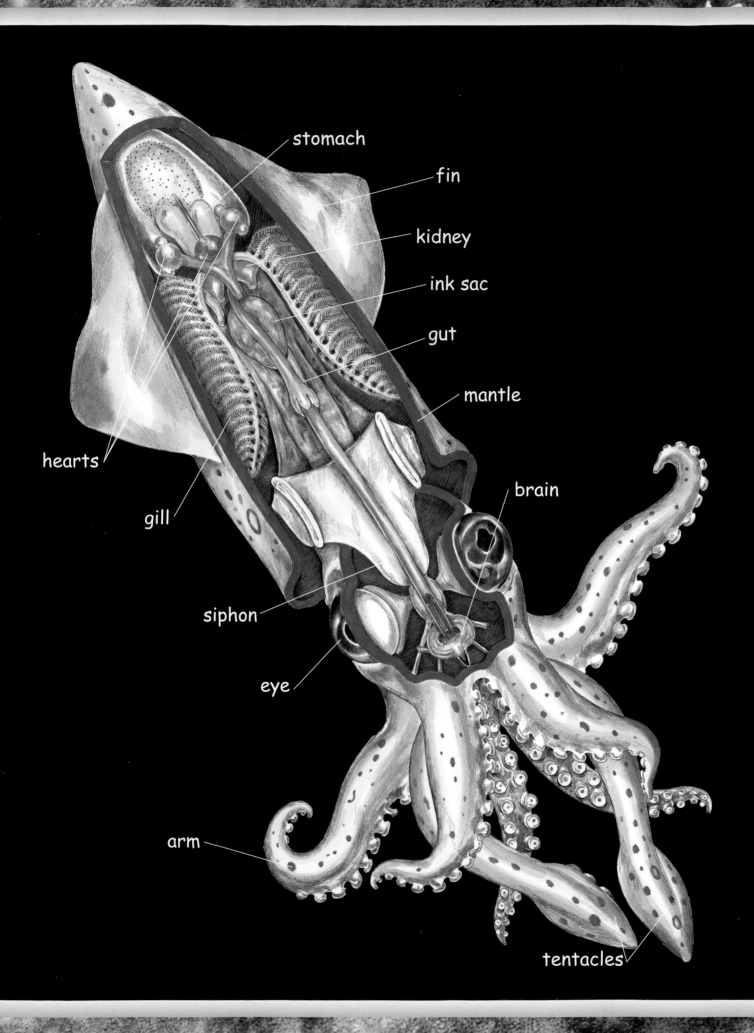

stomach

fin

kidney

ink sac

gut

mantle

hearts

brain

gill

siphon

eye

arm

tentacles

What's special about cephalopods?

Octopuses and squid are highly intelligent. They are able to learn, remember and solve problems. Their sensitive arms can tell them what they are touching even if they cannot see it. By altering the colour cells in their skin they can change their colour and patterns for camouflage, or display to show what mood they are in.

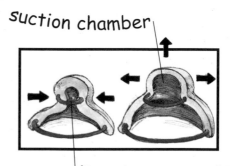

suction chamber

muscle contracting

A drawing showing how a sucker grips

Suckers are very sensitive. The brain sends messages to the sucker muscles, telling them to contract. This makes the suckers grip tightly.

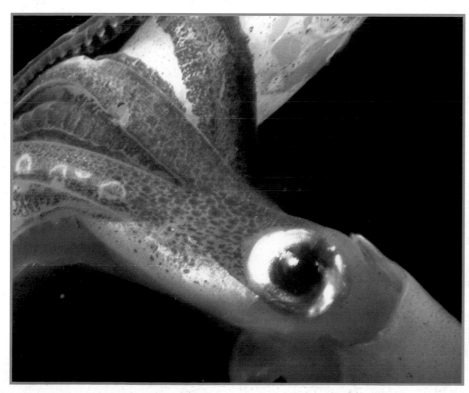

The eye of a squid

Did you know?

A cephalopod has some of the best eyes in the sea. Their eyesight is at least as good as a human's.

How do cephalopods reproduce?

Male octopuses and squid produce sperm in a packet, called a spermatophore. When it is time to breed, one of the male's arms carries this packet to the female. This arm is called the hectocotylus. It places the sperm mass inside the female's mantle cavity ready to fertilise her eggs when she lays them.

Two cuttlefish courting

Did you know?

Before mating, cephalopods display to one another using colour and movement. Displaying in this way helps the female to choose which is the best of several mates.

Cephalopods use rippling, changing patterns of body colour as their language. They communicate with each other in this way.

A male squid swims around its mate (right) displaying patterns of colour. This display identifies him and what he intends. It also wards off intruders and smaller males.

Two cuttlefish mate head to head (below). The male inserts his hectocotylus arm into the mantle of the female, placing the spermatophore inside.

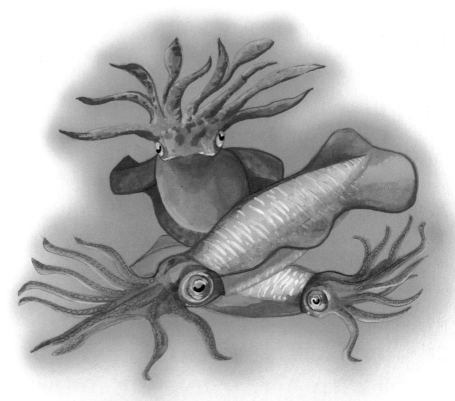

Are cephalopods good parents?

Female cephalopods lay hundreds of eggs. Squid and cuttlefish die soon after spawning, leaving the eggs to look after themselves. Octopuses lay from 150 to 400,000 eggs. The female cares for them, squirting them with oxygen-rich water and cleaning them with her arms. She helps them to hatch out of their egg cases. Once free the baby octopuses swim away.

Octopus egg cases

A shoal of squid laying their eggs together

Did you know?

A relative of the octopus, the paper-nautilus, has a special thin, chalky shell. She lays and cares for her eggs in this shell and sometimes the tiny male lives inside it, too.

Many species of squid shoal together (above) when it is time to mate and spawn. They even lay their eggs together, producing a huge pile. Cuttlefish lay their eggs alone in bunches which look like black grapes. After a storm at sea these are often washed up on the beach.

How large are cephalopods?

Cephalopods come in all sizes. Tiny sepiola cuttlefish are little more than a couple of centimetres and are found in rock pools. A wonder-lamp squid, found in much deeper water, is 4 cm long. Like a monster from the deep, the largest squid, a female Antarctic cranch squid, was caught off Antarctica in 2003. It was still only young, but its mantle measured 6 m long. These squid can live at a depth of 2,200 m.

Wonder-lamp squid shown actual size

Giant squid can weigh up to 900 kg. In 1878, an arm was found (probably a tentacle) measuring 10.7 m. Giant squid have the largest eyes in the animal kingdom – up to 25 cm across!

This diver (above) is shown to scale with an average-sized squid and a Atlantic giant squid with its hunting tentacles extended.

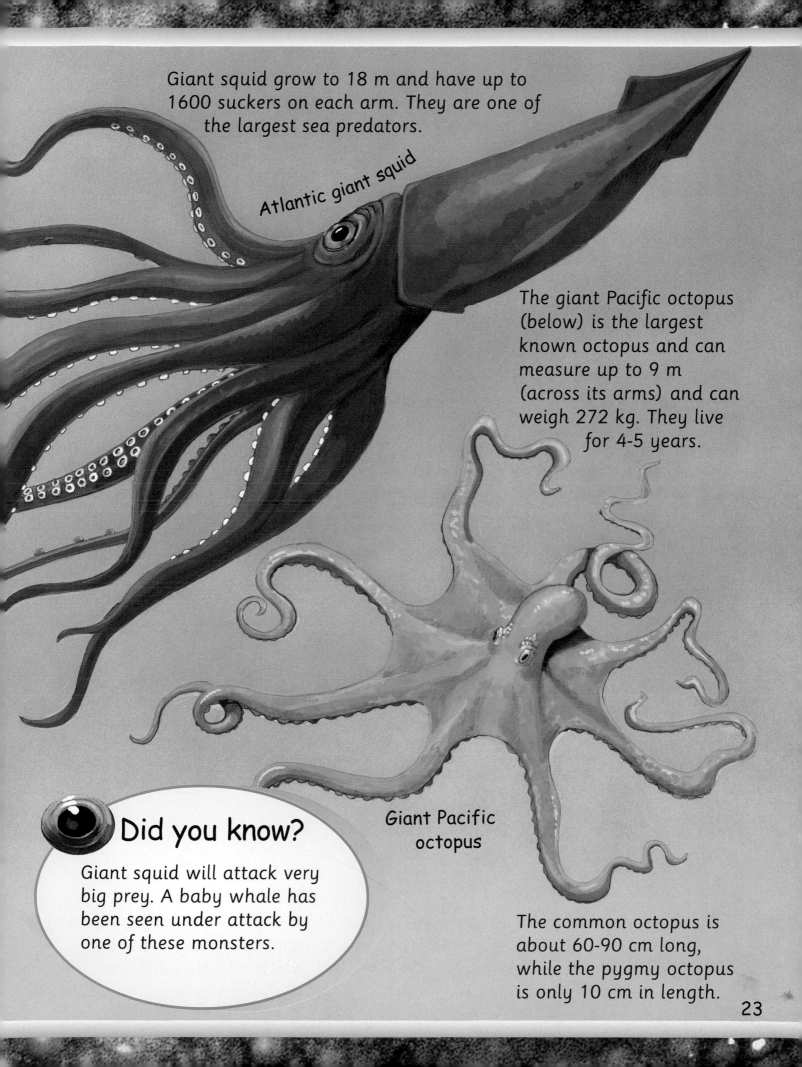

Giant squid grow to 18 m and have up to 1600 suckers on each arm. They are one of the largest sea predators.

Atlantic giant squid

The giant Pacific octopus (below) is the largest known octopus and can measure up to 9 m (across its arms) and can weigh 272 kg. They live for 4-5 years.

Did you know?

Giant squid will attack very big prey. A baby whale has been seen under attack by one of these monsters.

Giant Pacific octopus

The common octopus is about 60-90 cm long, while the pygmy octopus is only 10 cm in length.

What are the other cephalopods?

Cephalopods have been around for over 450 million years. Over 10,000 extinct species have been described, including ammonites and belemnites. There are over 650 species living today. The closest living relatives of octopuses and squid are the nautilus and the cuttlefish.

Ammonites

Hundreds of millions of years ago the ammonite (left) jetted the ancient seas. They had an armoured shell and were one of the most common sea creatures.

Cuttlefish

Cuttlefish (right) have a chalky internal skeleton supporting their body. It also acts as an internal lifebuoy. When they die this is often washed up on the beach.

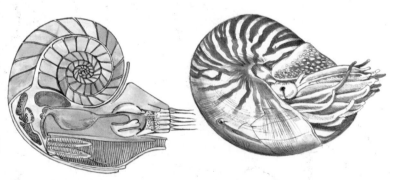

Nautiluses

Nautiluses are the only cephalopods that live inside a shell. This is made of several chambers. The animal lives inside the first and the others are full of gas and are used to control buoyancy.

Did you know?

Sepia ink from cuttlefish (below) is used for drawing. For this reason, cuttlefish are sometimes known as 'sepia'.

Do cephalopods have enemies?

Cephalopods are eaten by all kinds of creatures, including fish like sharks, and even other cephalopods. Birds such as penguins and albatross will pluck them from the sea. Mammals including seals, sea lions, whales and humans also like to eat them. If attacked they squirt ink to confuse their attacker. They are tough survivors and can even re-grow arms that have been bitten off.

Commercial fishing involves using all kinds of nets (below).
top: Trawling for sea-floor-dwelling animals.
bottom: A 'purse seine' net is laid around a shoal and then closed.

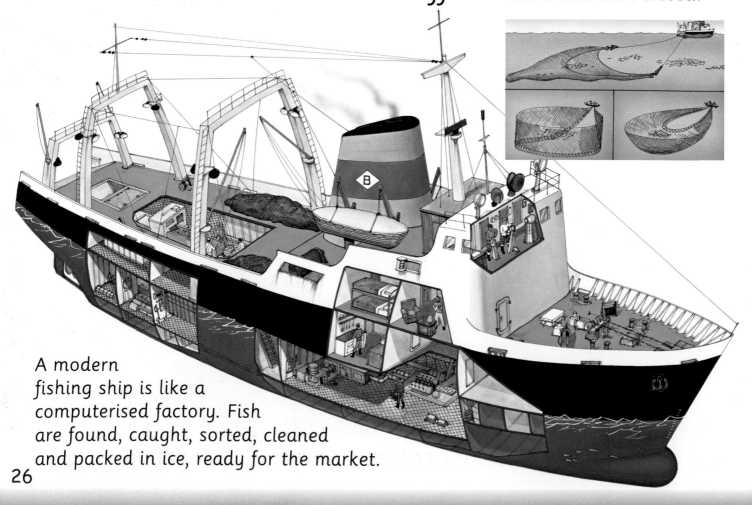

A modern fishing ship is like a computerised factory. Fish are found, caught, sorted, cleaned and packed in ice, ready for the market.

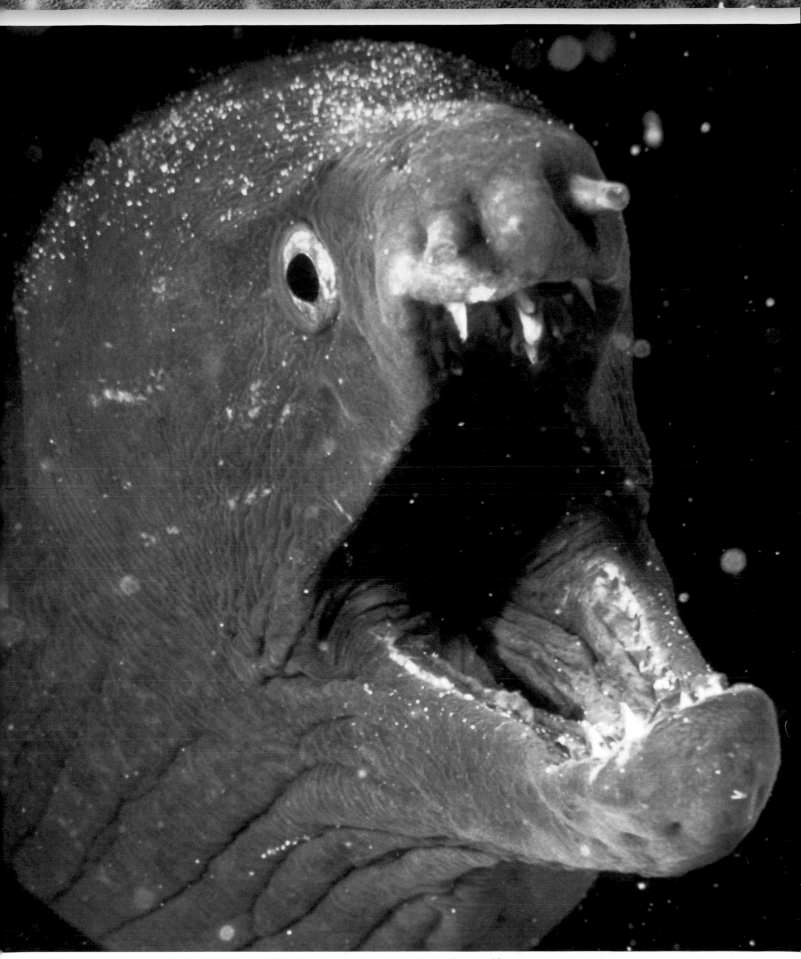

A moray eel is one of the octopus's deadliest enemies

Cephalopods around the world

Octopus and squid and their cephalopod relatives are found in all the seas and oceans. They live in shallow water on the shore down to depths of over 5000 m.

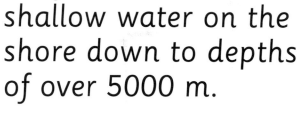

Robust clubhook squid

North Pacific squid are commonly caught on a large scale and eaten by humans.

There are 369 species of squid worldwide. Some live at great depths during the day and swim to the surface at night to feed.

Caribbean reef squid

North Pacific giant octopus

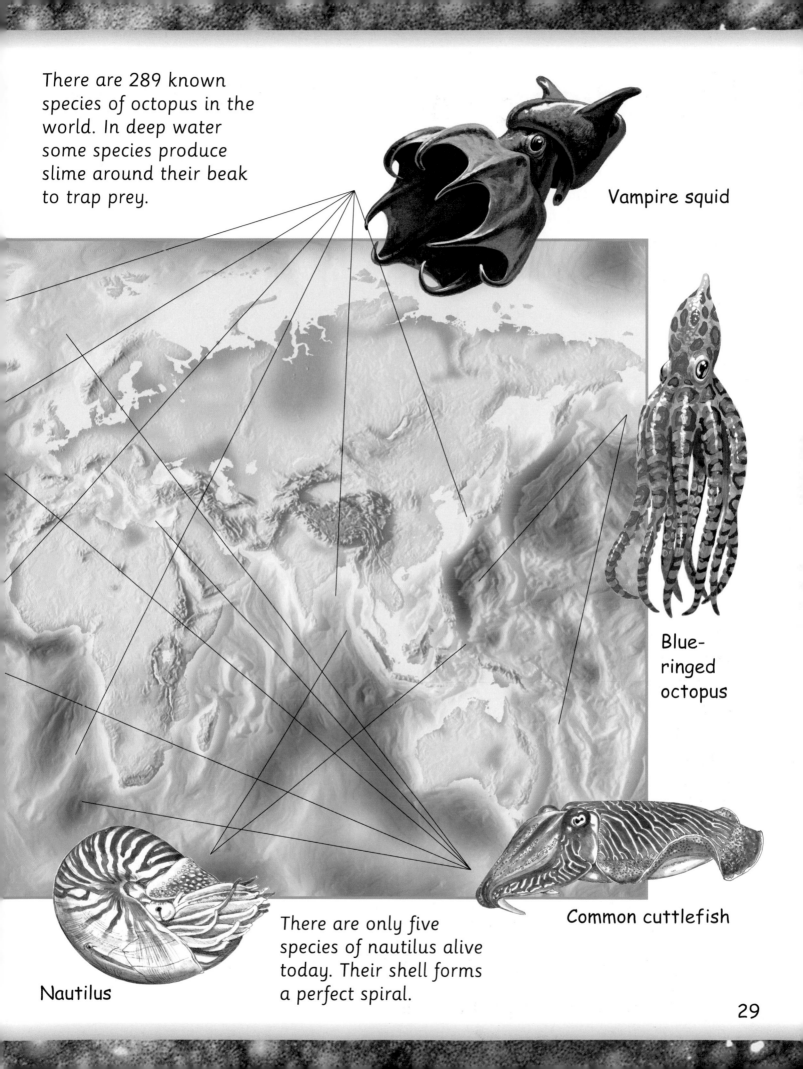

There are 289 known species of octopus in the world. In deep water some species produce slime around their beak to trap prey.

Vampire squid

Blue-ringed octopus

Common cuttlefish

Nautilus

There are only five species of nautilus alive today. Their shell forms a perfect spiral.

Cephalopod facts

Although they have evolved to have no shell, some octopuses have the remnants of one inside their body.

The oldest an octopus can live is about 5 years, but most live only one or two years.

Cephalopods breed only once in their lifetime. Common octopuses lay 400-500,000 eggs at a time, but only one or two youngsters will survive.

Cephalopods have three hearts – one in each gill to pump blood through the gills and a third to pump blood around the body.

Octopuses can temporarily blind an attacker by squirting ink in their eyes.

Although some people think a squid has ten arms, it actually has eight, like an octopus. The other two are tentacles.

Cephalopods taste and feel with their suckers.

Squid are amongst the fastest sea creatures and can travel up to 33 kph.

The blue-ringed octopus is only 2-20 cm long and is more poisonous than the deadliest snake.

Some squid, living in the dark ocean, shoot out bursts of light to confuse enemies.

Octopus suckers are very strong – pearl divers have reported that they cannot move one that has fixed itself to a rock.

When one squid was cut open it was found to have eaten at least 21 other squid.

96 squid beaks were once found in the stomach of an emperor penguin.

In 2002, an incomplete specimen of a giant octopus was found weighing 61 kg and measuring 2.9 m in length

Cuttlefish shell is used to make metal polish and even as an cure for indigestion.

The largest ammonite fossil ever discovered measured well over 2 m in diameter.

A cephalopod's brain surrounds its gullet.

Glossary

buoyancy The ability to float in water.

camouflage A method of hiding by using colour and shape to disguise the body.

cephalopod A marine mollusc with arms attached to its head.

display Behaviour by animals to attract mates.

evolve To change gradually over thousands or millions of years.

extinct A type of animal or plant that no longer exists.

fossil The very old remains of a plant or animal.

gill An organ for breathing in water.

gonads Male and female reproductive tissues producing sperm or eggs.

hectocotylus arm An arm of a cephalopod that transfers the spermatophore from the male to the female.

immobilise To make something unable to move.

Kraken A legendary many-armed, octopus-like sea monster.

mantle The bag of skin and muscle that encloses a cephalopod's organs.

mollusc An animal with a soft body and often a hard outer shell.

nocturnal A creature that is active at night and rests in the daytime.

predator An animal that hunts and eats another animal.

prey An animal that is hunted and eaten by another animal.

siphon A cephalopod's special tube, also called the funnel, that squirts water out.

spawn A mass of fertilised eggs in water.

sperm Male sex cells that fuse with a female's egg to produce a new animal.

spermatophore A packet of sperm transferred from a male to a female.

tentacle In cephalopods, a special flexible arm-like structure used in hunting and then tucked away when not in use.

venom A poison produced by an animal to kill or immobilise its prey or defend itself.

visceral mass The mass of body organs of a mollusc.

Index